Swimming Across the Pool

Story by Jenny Giles   Illustrations by Claire Bridge

Yasmin liked swimming
with her friends from school.
At the end of every lesson,
Miss Lee would let the children
play games in the water.

Sometimes the best swimmers
in the class
had a race across the pool.
Yasmin's friend Sarah could swim fast.
She often won the race.

Yasmin wanted to swim
in the race, too.
But she could only swim
halfway across the pool.

Then she had to stop
and put her feet down,
because that was the only way
she could get some air.

Miss Lee showed the children
how to turn their heads to the side
and take in air.

But Yasmin could not do it
while she was swimming.

"You just need to practise
a bit more,"
Miss Lee told her.

Yasmin watched Sarah
swimming across the pool.
She said to herself,
"I'm going to try again."

Yasmin stood with her back
to the wall.
Then she pushed off with her feet
and started kicking
as hard as she could.
Her arms went over and over
as she moved along.
She was going fast!

But Yasmin needed some air.
"I won't stop!" she said to herself.

She turned her head
out of the water,
and this time, she got some air.
Then she kicked even harder.

She could see the wall
just ahead of her.
She was nearly there!

Yasmin got to the other side
of the pool.
She was so proud of herself!

Yasmin stood up
and looked for Sarah.

But Sarah was swimming
to the other end of the pool.
And Miss Lee was talking
to one of the boys.

Yasmin didn't think
that anyone had seen her
swimming across the pool.

13

But Miss Lee **had** seen Yasmin!
She said to the class,
"It's nearly time
to get out, everyone!
We will just have a race
for the children
who can swim across the pool.
And I think someone else
is going to do it today!"

Yasmin smiled at Miss Lee.
Then she went to stand by Sarah.